London

THIS IS A CARLTON BOOK

Text and Design copyright © 2002 Carlton Publishing Group

This edition published by Carlton Publishing Group 2002
20 Mortimer Street
London
W1T 3JW

A CIP catalogue for this book is available from the British Library.

ISBN 1 84222 638 X

Commissioning Editor: Claire Richardson
Design: Adam Wright/Simon Mercer
Picture research: Claire Gouldstone
Production: Janette Burgin

Printed in Dubai

London

DAVID LITTLEFIELD

CARLTON
BOOKS

In 1945 London was a mess.

The rot had begun to set in five years earlier when German bombing raids left the city's East End cratered and covered in a veneer of dust. By the end of the Second World War vast tracts of the city had been flattened. There were holes in the Houses of Parliament and almost every other landmark building in London. The city had not undergone such wholesale destruction since the calamity of the Great Fire nearly three centuries earlier, only this time the capital was also bankrupt, war-weary and exhibiting all the symptoms of terminal decline. Author and London historian Peter Ackroyd wrote:

"London, THEN, WAS DRAB. COMPARED WITH OTHER GREAT CITIES, SUCH AS ROME AND PARIS AND NEW YORK, IT WAS UGLY AND FORLORN; FOR THE FIRST TIME IN ITS HISTORY IT HAD BECOME SOMETHING OF AN embarrassment."

The war sent London down new architectural paths, closing the door on what had effectively been a Victorian city. More than anything else it represented a chance for progressive architects to make their mark on a streetscape which was characterised by two main building styles – Gothic (Westminster Abbey, St Pancras Station) and Classical (St Paul's, Buckingham Palace). Architects had long argued over the relative merits of each approach, but the heat went out of the row in the early twentieth century when a collection of European architects developed a style that came to be known as Modernism.

Modernism was a problem for the reactionary British because it challenged the establishment on both social and aesthetic grounds. It was an international, rectilinear style of glass and concrete that embraced mass-production and had little respect for local traditions; and, it was supposed to help create a new, classless world order by providing a rational architecture that could accommodate everyone. Everyone, that is, except the conservative British. By 1945, there were only a handful of modern buildings in London – the High Point flats in Highgate and the Finsbury Health Centre in Clerkenwell, for example.

But the with war's end came the need for renewal, and the political agenda of Modernism seemed less distasteful. Apart from that, labour was scarce and building skills were in short supply, leading to the conclusion that perhaps mass-production really was the future of the building industry. By the early 1950s London had embarked upon a construction programme which would both invigorate and devastate the city. It's true that many buildings did not prove to be a success, and many unpopular residential blocks have now been pulled down. But architects needn't shoulder all the blame: build quality was often poor and local authority managers neglectful. The last half century has proved to be a hotbed of architectural invention – with all the highs and lows that experimentation entails. This book will examine some of the key buildings that emerged in this dynamic period.

Renewal got off to a slow start. The most significant historical marker is the 1951 Festival of Britain, a government-sponsored party to celebrate both the end of the war and the centenary of the Great Exhibition under Queen Victoria. The Royal Festival Hall is the sole survivor of the South Bank event, but it was originally surrounded by a huge complex of pavilions including the 111-metre wide Dome of Discovery and the slender, 91-metre high Skylon techno-sculpture. The Skylon was, in fact, an engineering marvel and a joke circulated at the time comparing it with the state of the economy: "Just like modern Britain; no visible means of support."

The Festival Hall was London's first significant, public piece of modernist architecture. Designed by a team led by Sir Leslie Martin, the building is still a vibrant, popular and successful arts centre. Influenced by the ideas of architects such as Swiss architectural giant Le Corbusier and Russian émigré Bertold Lubetkin, the hall exhibits many of the features of classic 1930s Modernism. In other words, clean, white-walled volumes pierced by large expanses of glass and horizontal window slots, all jacked up on slender columns. But in a curious break from the modernist norm, the hall was given a curved roof, a feature which softens the angular composition of the building's facades: solid and void, stone and glass.

The Festival of Britain was not confined to the South Bank. Built to exhibit a new model of public housing, the Lansbury Estate in Poplar was an exercise in the art of the possible. Today it seems an unambitious scheme that looks rather ordinary. At the time, though, it boasted innovative features such as houses with kitchens at the front and the country's first pedestrian shopping precinct. Noteworthy, however, is the Catholic church of St Mary and St Joseph on Upper North Street, an imposing brick edifice designed by Adrian Gilbert Scott, brother of Giles (who designed Battersea power station and the traditional phone box), and grandson of George (St Pancras and the Albert Memorial). It was described at the time as a "sprawling lumpish mass", but what it lacks in grace, this brooding, bunker-like building makes up in power – this is a structure to put the fear of God into you. It's only light feature is the tiny conical green roof, which it wears like a party hat.

By 1951 Modernism had changed direction and the Festival Hall was dated as soon as it was built. Le Corbusier and his admirers were now designing massive housing blocks in heavy, rough concrete (in French: *beton brut*) that dominated their surroundings. This work gave rise to the term "New Brutalism" in Britain, a phrase which came to imply an austere style of architecture that made heavy use of industrial materials and sought to group buildings together in clusters. The style was also meant to reflect the tough and brutal nature, yet inherent closeness, of the British working class.

The parallel blocks of the 1955 Roehampton Estate close to Richmond Park are an early example of this approach, but a more refined and less slab-like solution is found in the cluster block of Keeling House in Bethnal Green. Designed by Sir Denys Lasdun, who tried to remain aloof from the Brutalist group, but was nonetheless influenced by its ideas, the building consists of four accommodation towers joined at the centre by a service core of stairs and lifts. This was an attempt to recreate the traditional working-class street in the air. Each dwelling is two storeys high and the arrangement of the blocks means there are no long empty corridors. By the 1990s the building had become neglected and unpopular with its council tenants. Recently, however, Keeling House has undergone a renaissance; its architectural pedigree and obvious sculptural merits have led to its protection by conservation body English Heritage, and a sensitive renovation is attracting wealthy, private owners.

Husband and wife team Peter and Alison Smithson are more typical of the Brutalist movement. Although their reputation was built on a 1954 school in Hunstanton, Norfolk, it is their far from brutal complex of buildings for the Economist for which they are best-known in London. Tucked behind the Ritz on St James's Street, this trio of buildings has become a classic example of how to build contemporary architecture in a traditional setting. Each block is of a different height and the corners have been shaved off to temper their modern lines. Perhaps more importantly, the entire complex has been clad in travertine stone, a more traditional option than concrete and one that weathers better. The Economist cluster also works because the buildings lack the uniformity that has come to be associated with modern architecture: the window sizes vary between the three blocks and they share a cosy, asymmetrical plaza. The buildings also meet the ground well, and the vents and ugly mechanical areas that characterise much contemporary architecture are absent.

While the Smithsons were designing the Economist scheme, Lasdun was working on a far more difficult site. The Royal College of Physicians had commissioned him to design a headquarters building in the south-east corner of Regents Park next to a nineteenth century, neo-classical terrace built by John Nash. Lasdun drew up a decidedly modern scheme which architect Edward Cullinan described as

"the finest THREE-DIMENSIONAL WORK OF ART IN THE CUBIST TRADITION IN THESE ISLANDS",

when he wrote Lasdun's obituary in the *Architects Journal* in 2001. The building is complex, using both the clean lines and white planes of classic Modernism, as well as a more organic technique. The college defies simple description because it presents a very different composition depending on where you stand. It is a quiet, sculptural form that has become significant as the point at which Lasdun began to work out his theory of building as landscape – an idea that would come to fruition fifteen years later in his National Theatre. Here, however, the built landscape manifests itself as the dark brick mass of the lecture theatre that grows out from the principle structure almost like a cancerous growth.

The National Theatre, begun in 1963 but not completed until 1976, is Lasdun's *piece de resistance* and a seminal example of British architecture. Composed of a series of layered spaces, Lasdun thought of the theatre as geological strata within a landscape. This metaphor works particularly well on the inside, where spaces interpenetrate and lead naturally from vast halls to very private nooks and niches, like a sequence of subterranean caves. It is a beguiling place and, in the absence of the theatre crowd, becomes an architecture of light and dark. It even has a tactile appeal, being constructed of concrete that still bears the mark of its wooden moulds. Lasdun joked that people liked to stroke the walls, but it is in fact true.

Importantly, the theatre has been better maintained than its older cousins next-door – music venues Queen Elizabeth Hall and the Purcell Room, opened in 1967, and the Hayward Gallery, completed a year later. This complex of buildings is undoubtedly the most brutal of Brutalist architecture in the capital, and the buildings have long weathered calls for them to be torn down. Weathering is, in fact, part of the problem and the structures bear the marks of decades of rain and pollution. They also lack the range of scale that is a feature of the theatre, which manages to combine monumental architecture with intimate spaces. The Haywood et al can belittle their visitors, offering blank walls and unfriendly exterior spaces. They work well on the inside, however, especially the Hayward whose staircases and coffered ceilings combine to create a sculptural quality that is rare in more recent construction.

It is this quality that prompted Peter Moro, one of the architects on the Festival Hall, to write a glowing review of the complex. He states:

"THIS BUILDING does not use THE ORTHODOX VOCABULARY CONSISTING OF WALLS, ROOFS, WINDOWS

AND SO ON, BUT IS AN **ARTICULATED PIECE** OF sculpture IN WHICH ROOFS AND WALLS ARE NOT SEPARATE UNITS BUT CAST IN ONE . . . THIS **PERVERSE REVERSAL** OF ARCHITECTURAL EXPRESSION HAS GIVEN THE BUILDING ITS unique character AND HAS RESULTED IN A COMPOSITION OF ORIGINALITY AND OF CONSIDERABLE VISUAL **EXCITEMENT**."

The most obvious example of building as landscape (even cityscape) is the Barbican centre, a mega-structure whose genesis lay in the 1950s but which wasn't completed until 1982. Designed by Chamberlin, Powell & Bon, the complex is not well-loved by Londoners, largely because it is easy to get lost in the maze of buildings, walkways and passages of this new urban quarter. It is also a piece of tough architecture that refuses to compromise with its context and, like the castle that once stood there, it's difficult to find your way in. Nevertheless, it is a fantastically successful space: its flats, housed in three towers 122 metres high, command high prices and its arts centre is world-class. The way to appreciate the Barbican is to forget it is a building. Think of it, instead, as a piece of the city – almost a medieval town. This is heroic architecture that is built to last, and it is more crafted than one might think. The rough texture of the granite-concrete walls, an architectural reference to the pitted surface of ancient and renaissance walls, was created by builders wielding heavy hammers.

By the 1980s two new architectural themes were beginning to emerge, High-tech and Postmodernism. The origins of the High-tech movement are difficult to define. High-tech buildings are characterised by their exposed structures, an architecture that celebrates its engineered qualities. Vents and mechanical systems are put proudly on display, and the structural integrity of the building is clear to see. Richard Rogers' Pompidou Centre in Paris, and more recently his Millennium Dome, are good examples. Some argue that medieval cathedrals, with their ranks of slender load-bearing columns and flying buttresses, are the prototypes of High-tech, while others point to Victorian railway stations and the Palm House at Kew Gardens. But contemporary practitioners would probably argue that they are simply cranking the industrial aesthetic of modernism up a notch. Put another way, if architecture was to benefit from mass-production and new technologies, why shouldn't it learn lessons from eminently successful products such as aircraft, space-capsules and industrial buildings?

An early example of this thinking is not a building at all, but the 1962 aviary at London Zoo, a vast prismatic structure designed by architect Cedric Price and engineer Frank Newby (who also worked on the Skylon). The bird-cage is not only remarkable for being large enough to allow its captives to get airborne; its structural integrity is also a marvel. Supported on just two points, the aviary is held aloft by a clever lattice of steel and high-tension cables. As a solid form the structure would appear remarkable even today, but as a translucent cage it is merely the ghost of a building.

London's flagship high-tech structure is undeniably the Lloyds building. Designed by Richard Rogers, this dramatic headquarters was completed more than 15 years ago but still manages to steal the thunder of newer buildings. The decision to commission Rogers was an enlightened one from a three hundred year-old institution, but it was a branding coup; rarely is an office building so firmly linked to its owner in the mind of the public. Inside it is vast and contains an atrium some 70 metres high. This is exactly the point, of course – services like lifts and stairs, as well as the structure of the building, are located on the outside. Even lavatory modules are plugged into the sides, giving the impression that the whole assembly is really a kit of parts to be reconfigured as necessary.

This aesthetic is rooted in the ideas of Archigram, a 1960s group of architects and students who took machine-age models to extremes by fantasising about buildings (and even cities) made of pods which could be rearranged and plugged in whenever necessary. Critic Reyner Banham tried to summarise the approach in 1965:

"WHEN YOUR house CONTAINS SUCH A COMPLEX OF

PIPING, FLUES, DUCTS, WIRES, LIGHTS, INLETS, OUTLETS, OVENS, SINKS,

REFUSE DISPOSERS, HI-FI REVERBERATORS, ANTENNAE, CONDUITS,

FREEZERS, HEATERS – WHEN IT CONTAINS SO MANY SERVICES THAT THE

HARDWARE COULD stand up by itself

WITHOUT ANY ASSISTANCE FROM THE HOUSE – **WHY HAVE A**

HOUSE TO HOLD IT UP?"

With the possible exception of the Millennium Dome, Lloyds is the building for which Rogers will be remembered (in the UK anyway), although he has continued to build elsewhere in the capital. The Channel 4 headquarters on Horseferry Road, finished in 1994, continues his trademark use of stainless steel, while an eighteen-storey office complex completed two years ago at 88 Wood Street has been dubbed "the firm's finest building", by the Royal Institute of British Architects. In a sense 88 Wood Street is a reversal of Roger's other buildings: instead of acres of steel, the architect has used ultra-clear glass that makes the building appear more skeletal than either Lloyds or Channel 4. By common consent, 88 Wood Street is put together extremely well. As well as precision architecture, this is building as product design.

Rogers is not the only proponent of the High-tech movement. His friend and rival Norman Foster, designer of the troubled Millennium footbridge which stretches between St Paul's and the Tate Modern, also plays a lead role. So does Nicholas Grimshaw, architect of the magnificent Eurostar terminal at Waterloo – a building which manages to reinterpret the glories of Victorian railway architecture without pasticing it. Grimshaw also built the chunky Sainsbury's store in Camden, whose muscular engineering at street level carries a roof that needs no internal support, leaving a column-free interior.

Grimshaw's Camden store was completed in 1988, in the middle of a period that history has shown to be a testing one for the architectural profession. In the nineteenth century architects had engaged in what came to be called "the battle of the styles", fought between adherents of Gothic and Classical practices. In the 1980s they were at it again, only this time it was between Modernists and Postmodernists.

Postmodernism was a reaction against the functional aesthetic which had come to dominate the architectural landscape. Taking their cue from abroad (mainly the US), architects began decorating their buildings in an attempt to reverse what they considered to be the alienating effects of Modernism. Giant egg-cups were incorporated into Terry Farrell's 1983 TV-AM building in Camden, for example. Classical forms such as columns and arches began to reappear, even as shallow facades to add interest to what might otherwise be a drab box – what critic William J. R. Curtis describes scathingly as

"SKIN-DEEP historicism".

But opinion is divided over the integrity of Postmodernism. Art historian Ernst Gombrich, in his authoritative work *The Story of Art*, argues that the movement offered light relief from the strait-laced practices of Functionalism.

"Decoration CAN BE TRIVIAL AND TASTELESS, BUT IT CAN ALSO GIVE US pleasure, A PLEASURE WHICH THE puritans OF THE MODERN MOVEMENT WISHED TO DENY THE PUBLIC," he wrote.

Postmodernism is not a good name for the movement – it describes what it is not, rather than what it actually is. Consequently, it is often difficult to be exactly clear whether a building is Postmodern or not. The sleek, over-sized classical temple of Marco Polo House, built on Queenstown Road in 1987, is definitely postmodernist. But Terry Farrell's office complex above Charing Cross station (1990) and his MI6 headquarters across the river on Albert Embankment (1993) are more subtle examples of the approach – they are contemporary without being high-tech or purely functional, chunky without the uncompromising features of high brutalism, they're somehow redolent of the past without being too obvious.

Postmodernism does not have to be big, chunky and brash. A more genteel example is the tiny Clore Gallery, built between 1980 and 1985 by Sir James Stirling, one of the greatest architects of his generation. It is a complex, even playful little building; as if a child's drawing of a house had found the confidence to materialise as a built form. For a building that occupies a sensitive site between the stone of Tate Britain and the brick of a Victorian hospital, it is a brave piece of work – bright green window supports, a multi-coloured interior and a roof-like opening cut through the wall as an echo of the pediment topping the entrance of the 1897 Tate next door. The gallery does not offer the minimalist austerity commonly associated with new art buildings either; instead, it offers surprise as pink handrails lead to handsome display spaces.

The Sainsbury Wing of the National Gallery does much the same job, but in quite another language. This is London's Postmodern building *par excellence*, and it forms a crucial part of recent architectural history. Plans to extend the gallery were revealed in 1984, but Prince Charles unexpectedly stirred things up by condemning the scheme as

"A MONSTROUS CARBUNCLE ON THE face OF A MUCH-LOVED AND elegant friend".

As a result, the largely glass proposal was dropped and American firm Venturi Scott Brown and Associates brought in to devise an alternative scheme.

VSBA had already carved out a position for themselves as theoretical architects – one of their ideas was that architecture was simply the art of

"THE decorated shed … ARCHITECTURE AS SHELTER WITH symbols ON IT".

Moreover, they argued, it didn't much matter what the symbols were, so long as they helped people form emotional attachments to a building. In the case of the Sainsbury Wing, it was clear that the original classical form of 1838 should provide the architectural palette for the extension.

But the Sainsbury Wing, completed in 1991, is not copycat architecture. In effect, the architects have taken the architectural language of the gallery next door and mashed it up, using it how and when it suits. Classical features have been dissected, exaggerated and juxtaposed against modern materials like black glass. The gallery also borrows tricks from the renaissance paintings that the building displays. The staircase is wider at the top than the bottom, warping the perspective so that it appears a relatively easy climb (because it looks nearer). Likewise, the narrowing ranks of paired columns leading to the sixteenth century painting *The Incredulity of St Thomas*, by Giovanni Battista Cima da Conegliano, seem to make the painting an extension of the building itself.

In a sense, Canary Wharf Tower also sits within the Postmodern canon. A 244-metre high tower in the city's former docklands, it is essentially a giant obelisk, a monolithic rectangle topped by a pyramid. In fact, it would have been more obelisk-like if US-based architect Cesar Pelli had got his way. Pelli wanted the tower to be slimmer and five storeys taller, but the developers paying for it had other ideas. As a striking icon of the regeneration of London's east end, the steel-clad building is a success, but up close it fails to offer much of interest. The vast lobby, dripping in granite, is the epitome of crass commercialism – ever so flashy but devoid of intellectual depth. Disappointingly, the newer towers nearby are not much better.

These are not London's first towers, of course, but they do represent the city's first cluster of tall buildings. In the 1960s and 1970s, tall buildings were built in isolation – Centre Point and the Telecom and NatWest towers – giving the city a fragmented skyline that has been described as "a mouth full of broken teeth".

The 189-metre high Telecom Tower near Fitzroy Square was London's first truly tall building. Completed in 1965, it is a curiosity, being both a significant London landmark and a structure almost devoid of grace. In fact, architect Eric Bedford attempted to disguise what is essentially a hefty concrete column by cladding it in glass, giving it the appearance of a narrow office block. Don't be fooled – the glass conceals nothing more than stairs, lifts and electrical equipment.

Next came Centre Point, a forty-storey tower at the junction of Tottenham Court Road and Oxford Street that achieved notoriety by remaining empty for the fifteen years after its completion in 1971. Centre Point has never managed to win a place in the hearts of the public, mainly because of the inadequate traffic and pedestrian system at its base. But the building does have its merits, and its surfaces boast a beautifully sculptural, textured quality. It remains controversial, though; even early in 2002 when London mayor Ken Livingstone told a House of Commons committee he thought Centre Point was an example of an "attractive" tall building, his remark was greeted with gasps of amazement.

Richard Seifert, architect of Centre Point, also designed the 183-metre NatWest Tower. This arguably gives him the distinction of making as much impact on the London skyline as Christopher Wren. Completed in 1981 the NatWest tower was at one time the tallest office building in Europe. But, unlike its older brother on Oxford Street, it was better received by the public, possibly because it was tucked away in the commercial centre of the city rather than dropped directly into a low-rise shopping district. By the mid-eighties, however, it became clear that the floors in the tower (whose plan corresponded roughly to the form of the bank's triangular logo) were too small for the electronic dealing rooms being demanded by the booming financial services industry. They were also too close together to provide adequate space for miles of underfloor cabling. Centre Point suffered from the same problem, leading to a rash of new office buildings in the city, as well as new business centres in the Docklands and at Broadgate.

After twenty years the NatWest Tower, now vacated by the bank and renamed Tower 42, is still the tallest structure in the City. Its supremacy will not even be challenged by Norman Foster's extraordinary building for insurance firm Swiss Re, set for completion during 2003. Nicknamed the "erotic gherkin", the curved surfaces of this 180-metre high tower will channel currents of air inside the building to act as a natural alternative to air conditioning.

The gherkin is part of a wave of exciting new architecture breaking across London. Prompted by millennial celebrations, Lottery money has been poured into grand arts projects while private clients appear to be persuaded of the benefits of contemporary design. The NatWest Media Centre at Lord's Cricket Ground set the millennial pace in 1999. Built for journalists and broadcasters covering the game, this curvaceous, shiny building almost floats above the cricket ground like a giant eye. Designed by adventurous practice Future Systems, the centre is made from sheets of aluminium, shaped and welded together by boat-builders. Winning the prestigious Stirling Prize in 1999, the judges called it:

"a complete one-off... AN ARCHITECTURAL BREATH OF FRESH AIR". And it certainly is.

Postmodernism seems to have gone away for the moment, leaving High-tech (or versions of it) as the temporary winner in the on-going debate between form and function. The London Eye, Peckham Library, the new Greater London Authority head-quarters and the much-maligned Millennium Dome are all examples of architects embracing the possibilities that technology can offer. The complex curves of Foster's magnificent roof covering the British Museum's Great Court, for example, were conceived with the help of software used for aircraft design. And the Teflon roof of the Dome weighs less than the air it contains.

Two buildings are worth picking out as exceptions to the norm: the British Library and Tate Modern. The British Library finally opened its doors in 1998 after thirty-five years of design work, political manoeuvring and even a change of site. Again dismissed by Prince Charles, who slammed it as "an academy for secret police", the building is far more elegant and welcoming on the inside than on the out. Set back off the Euston Road behind a formidable wall and cumbersome gates, the heavy massing and vaguely nautical lines of this building can appear intimidating to the casual observer but the interior opens out into a surprisingly light-filled and well-crafted atrium. Unfortunately for architect Colin St John Wilson, the planning authority insisted that he match the materials of the gothic St Pancras station next door, but the expanses of brick and slate make the library look uncomfortably like the vastly inferior superstores being built by supermarket chain Tesco.

Tate Modern, on the other hand, is a contemporary interior within an existing brick structure. Designed as Bankside power station by Giles Gilbert Scott in 1948, the building lay unused from 1982 to 2000 when it re-opened as a centre for contemporary art. Masterminded by Swiss firm Herzog & de Meuron, the aesthetic of the original building was preserved and even the new seven-storey interior structure was given a heavy, industrial treatment. Curiously, the architects chose to locate the main entrance not on the river-front under the chimney but around the corner on the western side of the building. What this does, however, is provide the visitor with a breath-taking vista running the entire length of what was once the turbine hall of the power station. The building has proved to be immensely popular as a tourist attraction and visitor numbers have far exceeded expectations. Fortunately, only two-thirds of the building has been converted, so there is plenty of room for expansion.

London is littered with idiosyncratic buildings that buck the trend. The magnificent Shri Swaminarayan Mandir temple built by the local Hindu community in Neasden in 1995, and the Globe Theatre which has been reconstructed in authentic Elizabethan style on the South Bank, are examples of architecture as cultural memory. Not all new architecture is as daring as it might be because architects have to contend with the context of a historic city; but a high regard for ancient neighbours can lead to inadequate and compromised architecture. The developers replacing the sixties complex at Paternoster Square to the north of St Paul's, for example, are so anxious to respect the cathedral next door that the new buildings will be merely polite. It is worth remembering that, in its day, St Paul's was itself controversial – even well into the construction programme, most of the public expected it to be topped with a traditional spire rather than a "popish" dome.

Having said that, London's architecture is in excellent health. You need only pass through the new tube stations on the Jubilee line to see what can be achieved when architects are allowed to let rip. And there are plenty of bold projects waiting in the wings: Wembley and Arsenal football stadiums are to be replaced, while a world-class team of architects is lined up to turn Battersea power station into the centrepiece of a whole new district of south-west London. There are even plans afoot to construct an extraordinary new extension at the Victoria and Albert Museum and an immense 300-metre "shard of glass" office complex at London Bridge. Some of these schemes won't be finished for another decade, and what happens after that is anyone's guess.

There is nothing certain about architecture. But what you can be sure of is that buildings which are controversial today stand every chance of being revered tomorrow. New structures will continue to be both a response to emerging technologies and a nod to the past. And London, home to two thirds of the UK's architects, will be where most of it will happen.

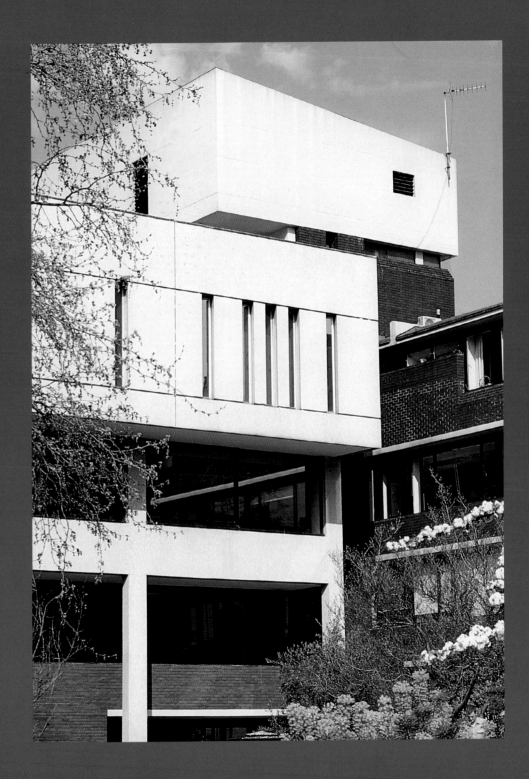

and let thy feet
millenniums hence
be set in midst of knowledge

GREAT COURT, BRITISH MUSEUM

Norman Foster's spectacular roof over the British Museum's Great Court. The curving structure incorporates 3300 glass triangles.

PECKHAM LIBRARY, INTERIOR

Wil Alsop's Peckham Library, a multi-coloured construction which won the £20,000 Stirling prize for architecture in 2000.

CANARY WHARF TUBE/MI5 BUILDING

Foster's tube station at Canary Wharf in London's Docklands, a grand, cavernous structure in concrete (left). Terry Farrell's Postmodern MI5 building (right).

SAINSBURY WING, NATIONAL GALLERY

Clever space planning and the use of perspective at the National Gallery's Sainsbury Wing allows some paintings to appear as though they are extensions of the building.

INTERIOR, ROYAL COLLEGE OF PHYSICIANS

The Royal College of Physicians, a brilliant Modernist composition near Regents Park by Denys Lasdun.

ROYAL FESTIVAL HALL

The Royal Festival Hall, the centrepiece of the 1951 Festival of Britain, was London's first large public building to employ the Modernist style.

ROYAL COLLEGE OF PHYSICIANS

Lasdun's Royal College of Physicians combines the lines and planes of Modernism with a more organic form in its curving, brick lecture theatre.

NATIONAL THEATRE/HAYWARD GALLERY

Lasdun's *piece de resistance*, the Royal National Theatre (left). The concrete forms of the controversial Hayward Gallery – numerous campaigns have been launched to pull it down (right).

THE BARBICAN

The Barbican, a city within the City, employs a rugged form to accommodate popular apartment blocks, new public spaces and a world-class arts centre.

LLOYDS

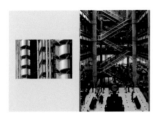

Richard Rogers' Lloyds building of 1986. The capital's best example of High-tech architecture where much of the structure and servicing is found on the building's exterior.

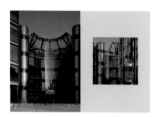

CHANNEL 4

Roger's Channel 4 building in Victoria, another High-tech structure with a remarkable, curving glass wall. As with Lloyds, lifts race up the outside of the building.

MILLENNIUM BRIDGE

Norman Foster's steel and aluminium Millennium Bridge, which was closed for nearly two years after it wobbled dramatically on its opening in summer 2000.

EUROSTAR TERMINAL

Nicholas Grimshaw's Eurostar Terminal at Waterloo is a glorious contemporary interpretation of Victorian railway architecture.

TV-AM

Farrell's 1983 TV-AM building in Camden, a fun Postmodern building which incorporated giant egg-cups into its structure.

CHARING CROSS

Farrell's office over Charing Cross station, a Postmodern building of steel and granite and a dramatic addition to the Thames upon completion in 1990.

MI6

Farrell's cream-coloured MI6 head office set on the riverbank in Vauxhall – a formidable, bunker-like building for the country's intelligence services.

CLORE GALLERY, TATE BRITAIN

James Stirling's Clore Gallery, a Postmodern addition to the Tate Britain completed in 1985. This is a playful building that resembles a child's drawing sprung to life.

SAINSBURY WING, NATIONAL GALLERY

Venturi Scott Brown and Associates' Sainsbury Wing extension to the National Gallery in Trafalgar Square. This classicist interpretation followed a more contemporary design which was rubbished by Prince Charles.

CANARY WHARF TOWER

Cesar Pelli's Canary Wharf tower, a steel-clad icon of the regeneration of London's docklands. A monolithic rectangle topped by a pyramid.

CENTRE POINT/TELECOM TOWER

The 40-storey Centre Point tower over Tottenham Court Road tube station – a sculptural building which created a poor traffic and pedestrian system at its base (left). And the graceless Telecom Tower, built in 1965 (right).

TOWER 42

The NatWest Tower, now called Tower 42, built by Richard Seifert – the architect responsible for Centre Point. This was a more successful structure, a form inspired by the logo of the bank which commissioned it.

NATWEST MEDIA CENTRE

Future System's aluminium NatWest Media Centre at Lord's Cricket Ground, winner of the 1999 Stirling Prize, which was assembled by boat-builders.

LONDON EYE

The London Eye, by architects Barfield Marks, is an extraordinary structure that is universally admired. Originally granted planning permission for just five years, the Eye is likely to become a permanent fixture.

PECKHAM LIBRARY

Alsop's Peckham Library, a quirky building clad in coloured glass and copper, is so popular that library attendance in Southwark has soared.

MILLENNIUM DOME

The controversial Millennium Dome by Richard Rogers. Although the contents received mixed reviews, the Dome itself is an engineering marvel.

GREAT COURT, BRITISH MUSEUM

Foster's Great Court, built around the drum of the British Museum's nineteenth-century reading room, which is now open to the general public for the first time in its history.

BRITISH LIBRARY

Colin St John Wilson's British Library at St Pancras. This forbidding structure opens out into a sequence of glorious, light-filled spaces inside.

TATE MODERN

Tate Modern – Giles Gilbert Scott's former power station that has been converted into a highly popular contemporary art gallery by Swiss architects Herzog & de Meuron.

CANARY WHARF TUBE STATION

Norman Foster's sublime Canary Wharf tube station on the Jubillee Line, built in a former dock, which is as long as the Canary Wharf tower is high.

GLA HEADQUARTERS/SWISS RE TOWER

Foster's GLA headquarters (left) and a computer-generated image of the tower due to be built for insurance company Swiss Re (right). The curves of these high-tech buildings are beginning to have a dramatic impact on London's skyline.

Picture credits

The publishers would like to thank the following sources for their kind permission to reproduce the pictures in this book:

Bibliography

– "London, then, was drab . . . ."

   London, The Biography, Peter Ackroyd (Chatto & Windus, London 2000).

– "the finest three-dimensional work of art ..." *The Architect's Journal*, 18.1.01, p24

– "This building does not use the orthodox vocabulary consisting of ..."

   The Architect's Journal Centenary Issue 9.3.95, EMAP Business Publications

– "When your house contains such a complex of piping ..."

   Modern Movement in Architecture, by Charles Jencks. Penguin 1987.

– "skin deep historicism" *Modern Architecture Since 1900* William JR Curtis (Phaidon, 2001)

– "Decoration can be trivial and tasteless ..." *The Story of Art*, EH Gombrich (Phaidon, 1996)

– "the decorated shed...architecture with symbols on it" *Learning From Las Vegas*, Robert Venturi, Denise Scott Brown & Steven Izenour (MIT Press, 1988)